Surviving & Thriving After the L

14 EFFECTIVE WAYS TO HEAL AFTER PERSONAL LOSS

TECORA HARVEY

Copyright © 2020 Tecora Harvey

All rights reserved. No part of this book may be reproduced, stored, or transmitted by any means- whether auditory, graphic, mechanical, or electronic- without written permission of both publisher and author, except in the case of brief excerpts used in critical articles and certain other noncommercial uses permitted by copyright law. Unauthorized reproduction of any part of this work is illegal and is punishable by law.

Because of the dynamic nature of the internet, any web addresses or links contained in this book may have changed since publication and may no longer be valid. The views expressed in this work are solely those of the author and do not necessarily reflect the views of the publisher, and the publisher disclaims any responsibility for them.

Library of Congress Control Number: 2020920643

ISBN 13: 978-0-578-78544-8 (Paperback)

ISBN 13: 978-1-7364049-0-4 (E-Book)

ISBN 13: 978-1-7364049-1-1 (Audiobook)

Editing by: Speak Write Play, LLC

Book Cover Design by: Camden Lane Creative Agency

Interior Infographic: Tecora Harvey

Back Cover Photography by: Marvie Wright Photography

Printed in the United States of America

ORDERING INFORMATION:

Special discount available on large quantity purchases by corporations, associations, and others. For details, visit www.tecoraharvey.com

Visit www.tecoraharvey.com
For additional resources to aid your healing.

DEDICATION

To my angel, Pearlie Mae, you took on the challenge of raising your granddaughter as your own.

Thank you for being the epitome of strength, endurance, selflessness, and perseverance.

ACKNOWLEDGMENTS

God, thank You for every blessing, miracle, experience, loss, failure, path, and person You knew was leading me to *Surviving & Thriving After the L: 14 Effective Ways to Heal After Personal Loss*.

I am beyond grateful for the once-in-a-lifetime opportunity to work with a coach who lives and breathes encouraging other women to write, speak, and walk in their purpose. Thank you Jasmine Womack and the entire Author Made Easy family.

This book would not have been born without a strong dream team. I'm sending hugs to mine. Editor, I appreciate your telling-it-like-it-is approach, expertise, and sweet spirit. You are truly a gem. Book Cover Designer, your creative mind and amazing energy is astounding; thank you for being so vibrant.

My children, I am more than favored by being your mom. Each one of you has a bright personality and talents that make me smile and laugh daily. Thank you for motivating me to always bring my A game. Thank you for being a constant reminder that life is precious and miraculous. Thank you for continuing to teach me that there is so much joy still to come.

To the amazing man God allowed me to meet, thank you for supporting my dream and vision from the jump. Thank you for being positive and encouraging each time I said I wanted to but didn't know how. Thank you for your unconditional love, support, and sacrifice, as well as for holding it down while I embarked on my creative journey.

To the amazing group of women who I have been fortunate enough to connect with online, thank you for being a source of inspiration, shining brightly, and showcasing all of your Black Girl Magic.

To all of my family and friends, I appreciate your love, support, and encouragement. Thank you for sowing into me and being in my corner.

TABLE OF CONTENTS

INTRODUCTION... viii

PART ONE
RE-ESTABLISH A STRONG
SPIRITUAL FOUNDATION... *1*

CHAPTER ONE
D-A-I-L-Y PRAYER & MEDITATION HABITS... 2

CHAPTER TWO
HOLD YOURSELF ACCOUNTABLE... *10*

CHAPTER THREE
INCORPORATE ACTS OF GRATITUDE INTO YOUR
DAILY ROUTINE... *17*

PART TWO
THERAPY IS FOR YOU... *23*

CHAPTER FOUR
WORK WITH A PROFESSIONAL... *24*

CHAPTER FIVE
THE TYPE OF THERAPY MATTERS... *33*

CHAPTER SIX
BE CONSISTENT... *37*

CHAPTER SEVEN
INVESTING IN YOUR MENTAL HEALTH... *40*

SURVIVING & THRIVING AFTER THE L

PART THREE
SET HEALTHIER BOUNDARIES... *45*

CHAPTER EIGHT
DON'T BE ACCESSIBLE 24/7... *46*

CHAPTER NINE
NO MORE PEOPLE PLEASING... *49*

CHAPTER TEN
STOP APOLOGIZING... *52*

CHAPTER ELEVEN
YOU ARE YOUR OWN EXPERT... *55*

PART FOUR
INDULGE IN SELF-CARE... *59*

CHAPTER TWELVE
GET CLEAR ON WHAT REALLY BRINGS YOU JOY... *60*

CHAPTER THIRTEEN
HEALTH IS NON-NEGOTIABLE... *63*

CHAPTER FOURTEEN
QUALITY VS. QUANTITY... *67*

TECORA'S FAVORITE GO-TO RESOURCES... 71

EPILOGUE... 73

INTRODUCTION

Hey, lady! I am excited that you have purchased *Surviving & Thriving After the L: 14 Effective Ways to Heal After Personal Loss*! Since you're reading this book, you are likely in a place where you desire a better quality of life but aren't sure where to start or how to take your next steps.

Many women, especially African Americans, aren't aware that self-care is an option to them or how to prioritize it. We, including myself, don't always connect how vital self-care is to our healing process and mental health. This book was written to encourage and compel you to heal, thrive, and embrace change after experiencing trauma or personal loss.

Oftentimes, **life** happens. We find out, after the fact, that we are ill-equipped or lack the proper coping skills to handle what gets thrown in our paths. It's similar to traveling and realizing, once you're miles away, that you didn't pack all the necessities for your trip. You have toothpaste, but there's no toothbrush to put it on. You have heels, but you forgot the gym shoes you'll need to go hiking.

My intention is that this book will be a resource and guide to assist you as you begin or continue your healing process. I desire for you to become happier, be bolder, and no longer get emotionally stuck. I want you to show up as your authentic self and take those next steps forward.

I am writing this book because I can relate to where you may be right now. In my own life, I have experienced multiple traumas and personal losses. When I was 10 years old, my mother committed suicide by consuming alcohol and swallowing a large quantity of sleeping pills. After that, I experienced bouts of depression because I lost a parent as a child. Sometime later, I found myself on the receiving end of domestic violence. Thankfully, I was able to get out and survive that situation. My next trauma came when my grandmother, the woman who raised me, passed. I've lived through and beyond the "death of a dream" a.k.a. divorce. From there, unemployment reached my door, and I found myself trying to figure out how to pay for basic needs and living expenses.

After going through several periods of **life** knocking the wind out of me, I learned to use the concepts I'm sharing with you in this book to regain my focus and come out on the other side. I know how and who to ask for help. I also know which boundaries to maintain so that I can continue my healing journey. Healing is a lifelong commitment.

By way of awareness, therapy, and large doses of self-care, I have been able to heal, shine, and thrive in the face of adversity. Because of this, I encourage and support other women throughout their healing journeys.

My aha moment came after going through divorce and being unemployed. I knew I wanted more control over my life to experience a deeper level of peace and prosperity. I also wanted to become the best mother I could to my children. Listen, once I let go of things that were not serving me, I was able to accomplish my own personal goals. I created my home-based business from a skill I already possessed, typing, while still working my 9 to 5. This book is a product of eliminating distractions, getting emotionally unstuck, forgiving myself for past failures, and committing to sharing what I have to offer with you.

Within the past year, I have been able to prioritize self-care and make it non-negotiable. As a result, I'm succeeding in my weight loss journey and becoming healthier from head to toe.

TECORA HARVEY

With less mental fog, I've even been able to grow my business during a global pandemic.

Surviving & Thriving After the L: 14 Effective Ways to Heal After Personal Loss details the effective strategies I implement on a daily basis to operate from a place of presence and persevere in spite of **life**'s roadblocks. I understand that you might be perplexed about how to adopt effective healing strategies to overcome past hurts, traumas, or personal losses. I want you to commit to the healing process and make your growth a priority.

I'm excited about your journey. After reading this book, you will no longer have to remain stuck when **life** dishes out whatever it wants at you or deals you a hand of misfortune. You will begin to jump over the hurdles and become a source of inspiration for someone else. No more looking in the rear-view mirror. Are you ready for the next step forward?

Happy Healing,

Tecora Harvey

Tecora Harvey

PART ONE
RE-ESTABLISH A STRONG SPIRITUAL FOUNDATION

CHAPTER ONE

D-A-I-L-Y PRAYER & MEDITATION HABITS

Listen, it's no accident that Part One of this book is about **re**-establishing a strong spiritual foundation. Like me, you may have learned about God and spirituality as a little girl. Prior to **life** happening, I had one level of faith and a prayer life that was often inconsistent, shaky, and circumstantial. If you can identify with where I was, you may realize that a mindset shift needs to occur but don't know where to begin. Establishing a strong spiritual and faith-based foundation is critical to beginning to heal from any personal loss. Consistent, intentional prayer and meditation will allow you to take your first or next steps forward. Each can provide a new level of acceptance and peace. You can go from constantly asking why to processing your grief, embracing **life**, and taking advantage of resources that are available to you.

In 2014, I was unemployed for a little less than a year. I was parenting alone, broke, busted, and disgusted. I mean, I had canned tomato soup and crackers for dinner a few times a week. When I did have a few dollars and could afford a burger from a fast food restaurant, I automatically asked for free ice water to drink. It got to a point where I overdrafted my checking account to buy groceries and put gas in my tank. At those moments, I only thought, *I'll have to figure it out later.* I was so broke that I'd go into a store to make a $4.99 purchase, give the cashier a $5 bill, then get mad when I didn't get my .01 cent back. At the time, this seemed like such a disrespectful and inconsiderate act, but I was in survival mode. You know, a place where you're simply solving problems one day at a time because you're too overwhelmed to think about anything else?

During this time, the next day's events were uncertain because I had no financial stability and lived in fear about the outcome of almost every decision I made. I felt guilty if I bought a large coffee that was .50 cents or so more than the small. I felt guilty when I had to tell my children that we couldn't donate treats to their class celebrations. I'd wake up in the middle of the night thinking about saving gift cards I received instead of spending the money on our basic needs. I was frustrated. Not knowing what else to do, I had to rely on getting up every day and preparing my mind for what was ahead. I began to wake up early, a little bit earlier than my children, to pray. Although it may not seem like much, this was a way for me to get clarity about what direction to take on that particular day. Honestly, it helped me a lot.

To say that 2014 was tough for me would be an understatement. I can recall days when I opened the mail and found a pile of bills, most of which I could not pay. I'd review loan statements and the interest that was accruing, then immediately feel a sense of hopelessness. It got to a point where I'd bring the mail in, continue to let it collect in one pile, but never open anything. Have you ever done this? I was never prideful, but I had been self-reliant and felt uncomfortable asking for financial help. I quickly learned to eat humble pie. "Can I borrow" became one of my monthly phrases as I was compelled to eventually reach out to close friends and family for assistance.

One morning, on the way to drop one of my daughters off at school, she told me she needed $5 to buy some things from the bake sale. I remember yelling at her saying, "Stop, telling me these things at the last minute! You just assume I have money. I don't have $5. If you had told me days ago, I could have put together some change or figured out how to get you the money!" My daughter walked into her elementary school so disappointed. I remember her walking to the car at the end of the day with a smile on her face because one of her friends treated her to some desserts from the bake sale.

Because I didn't have to worry about finances prior to 2014, I wasn't prepared when things took a turn for the worse. At this particular moment in my life, when everything was on me and I had limited funds to pay for it all, it was like I transformed into someone else. During this time, if anyone called me to ask for, talk about or, collect money, I developed an instant attitude with that person. I woke up every day attempting to solve my cash flow issues. Most days, being completely honest, I went to bed defeated by failed efforts to solve my financial problems.

Aside from a bout of unemployment, my divorce was finalized in 2014. I'm of the opinion that chaos, frustration, irritability, upset, discomfort, fear, and grief are normal emotions that come with the territory. Oh, the stress of it all. My divorce provided an opportunity to start new. With two suitcases full of belongings, I removed myself and my children from an unhealthy environment. There were many nights I stayed awake in bed talking to God. I told Him, "If you just deliver me, I don't care if I have nothing. Just deliver me, God. I'm tired. I can't do this anymore. I know that the kids will be okay." God answered my prayers, and I was cool with starting life from scratch. It meant finding a new place to live, getting a new source of transportation, setting up new latchkey arrangements for my children, learning to budget with one income, and other things that came with restarting life from ground zero. Even though it was hard, it didn't matter because peace is priceless.

My social life also took a hit during this time. I couldn't hang on to old friendships and relationships that were keeping me stuck. You know, the friend who tells you that you should have stayed in the relationship even after you'd gone into great detail about that same relationship leaving you with a quality of life that made living seem unbearable? There's also the relative who gives you twisted advice due to their own inability to heal because they've chosen to live a life of contentment by settling instead of pursuing a life of unspeakable joy. Finally, there are people who find entertainment in your pain. I had to let go of all of those types of people in my life because everyone deserves love. God does not mean for anyone to live in bondage, abuse, or misery.

One of the first things I did after my divorce was look for a new church home. Now, some people who get divorced can remain at the same church, but that was not my reality. I asked God for fresh friendships and a new worship environment. At that time, I needed to be around others who I knew had a strong spiritual foundation and could support me on my new journey. I desired to worship free of any judgments or unwarranted expectations from people who only saw one aspect of my married life. I was not in a place where I could handle ridicule from people who didn't know what I had to go through Monday through Saturday, so I made the best decision for myself and my children. It wasn't even leaving and going to a new church, but I knew everything needed to change if I wanted to experience complete healing.

Because I was basically restarting my life, I understood the need for more prayer and time with God in my life. I looked forward to surrounding myself specifically with prayer warriors who knew how to continually pray with and for me. Once I finally found that church, I knew that the members were people who would encourage and push me forward. If there was a period when I felt stuck, frustrated, hurt, or discomforted beyond belief, I knew that I was among believers who knew what God could do. Their faith and encouragement would help keep me focused in trusting God to intercede on my behalf on hard days. I appreciated texts or phone calls from my church community whenever they told me God placed me on their hearts or reminded me that they were praying for me.

When beginning to heal from past hurt, trauma, or personal loss, it is important to be around others who can uplift you. I have a friend who is one of the most peaceful people I've ever met. Over the years, I've watched this woman move gracefully through many challenges, tackle stress, and successfully navigate seasons of busyness. About five years ago, I began to notice that no matter what happened, despite how busy her day was, she always possessed a sense of happiness, peace, focus, and the ability to live in the present. Do you know someone like this? Curious to learn more about how my friend achieved this mental state, I asked her about her morning routine one day when we were both doing school pickups. She told me that she got up at least one hour before her family. During that time, my friend made it a point to do consistent weekly Bible studies and start her morning with prayer. I was amazed because I expected to hear a list of different steps and things she did to get ready for what was ahead.

In that conversation with my friend, I understood that she was intentional about preparing herself for what was to come. That discussion introduced me to the concept of mentally preparing for the day. Implementing a mental to-do list in my life would later be one of the best things I ever did. On the weekends, I began mapping out the events of each day in my planner. It had all sorts of markings, highlights, and stickers. I'm visual, so stickers excite me. You might be thinking, *Sis, that's what smartphones are for. You don't need a paper planner anymore. Just use a tablet.* I know. But, there's different strokes for different folks.

The schedule in my planner provided the framework of things that I wanted to accomplish daily, but it did not replace me getting up and centering myself before each day began. Similarly, the planner is not a substitute for you getting up and saying a prayer or participating in a morning routine to get ready for whatever comes your way. You can practice these habits if you have lost a parent, are unhappy with your position in life, are experiencing financial hardship, struggle with depression, have relationship issues, or feel like you're disconnected from the world.

If you prefer, you can also begin your day with a spiritual meditation. It's a great way to bring intentionality and calmness to your morning routine. There are different types of meditation, such as mantra, progressive relaxation, and movement. I am focusing on meditation for spiritual benefits in this chapter. Many women choose to meditate with essential oils like sage.

I recently saw a clip in Vogue Videos titled, *Alicia Keys's Guide to Wellness-Inspired Beauty, From How She Wraps Her Hair to the Skin-Care Secret That Gives Her That Glow.*[1] I was mesmerized by this video where Keys shared her early morning meditation practices. She starts her day early, and sometimes she works out.

---

[1] Ruffner, Zoe. "Alicia Keys's Guide to Wellness-Inspired Beauty, From How She Wraps Her Hair to the Skin-Care Secret That Gives Her That Glow." Vogue, 28 May 2020, https://www.vogue.com/article/alicia-keys-beauty-secrets-video.

TECORA HARVEY

Then, she heads to her bathroom, lights a candle, sets her intention for the day, and hydrates herself. I enjoyed the clip and chuckled learning that I'm not the only person who drinks from a water bottle in the bathroom. You can begin each day with a prayer or meditation for clarity, peace, patience, or focus. Finding yourself a good daily prayer or meditation journal can also help; I use a few interchangeably.

Over the years, as I dealt with trauma in my own life, there were times when I didn't get up early and mentally prepare myself for the day. I kind of just went with the flow. There was no direction or structure for the day, so things just happened. Because I wasn't intentional about setting clear goals for how I would spend my time, I was never satisfied with the day's events or results. I always felt overwhelmed or as if I was running behind. I wonder if this is the same for you. Have you had days where you really didn't know where to start or just couldn't focus?

I believe that you can tackle any L, or loss, once your emotions and mental state are balanced. I have a deep admiration for track and field. Runners prepare themselves just before a race begins by getting in their lane, placing their legs at 90 degrees, raising their bottoms, and keeping their heads down and backs straight. They must clear their minds and focus on the race in front of them. It's not always about where you are starting, the L you've experienced, or any odds not in your favor. You have to believe you can persevere and just **start**.

REFLECTION

Take a minute and assess where you are mentally and emotionally right now. Be honest. There is no shame. This is your starting position.

In the space below, write down some of your thoughts and date the entry. This will help you self-reflect later down the road.

What practices would you like to immediately incorporate into your morning routine to have more peace during the day?

_____

_____

_____

_____

_____

CHAPTER TWO
HOLD YOURSELF ACCOUNTABLE

You may have heard the word *accountability* mentioned in support groups. For instance, a person on the brink of relapse may be told to reach out to their *accountability* partner or sponsor. The term *accountability* is also often used in church sermons. Accountability simply means that you take responsibility for your actions or inactions; you commit to specific goals. An accountability partner is someone who encourages you to overcome challenges, struggles, and grief.

Tyler Perry's *The Single Moms Club*[2] is a movie about women holding one another accountable. In the film, all of the moms have children who attend the same school, and they meet while working on a fundraiser at the school. Nia Long's character, May, is a journalist raising her teenage son without the assistance of his father. In one scene, May is speaking to three of the other women about the struggles of being a single mom and suggests that they start their own support group. In response, the ladies band together to embrace and support one another, in their singleness, while parenting alone. The women cared for all the children like they did their own, became listening ears, and made themselves available for emotional support.

During the COVID-19 pandemic, I decided that I wanted to survive, work on being a better version of myself, and come out stronger. It reminded me of every L I've taken that had the

---

[2] *The Single Moms Club*. Written, Produced and Directed by Tyler Perry, performance by Nia Long, Tyler Perry Studios, 2014.

potential to paralyze me with fear. If you had asked me to define quarantine before the pandemic, I probably would have responded after reflecting on a scene from *Outbreak*, a 1990 thriller about the airborne Ebola virus. I would have previously said quarantine was what happened when someone with a contagious disease was put in a hospital room by themselves. I now know that quarantine can be associated with disease prevention, homeschooling, distance learning, working remotely, and being an essential worker.

Living under quarantine has caused feelings of anxiety, depression, grief, fear, and hopelessness for many people around the world. Enduring a pandemic and going into quarantine is quite traumatic and has resulted in personal loss for countless people globally. You may have lost a loved one, your employment, access to health care, financial stability, a relationship, the ability to have coffee meetups and visits with friends or relatives, or mommy breaks from your child(ren). Although you may think you are still bound to living in isolation because a lot of the world is under lockdown, I suggest switching your way of thinking.

If there was ever a time to get things done on my bucket list, it is during the pandemic that is still taking place as I write this book. Refusing to let the quarantine period keep me from being productive, I decided to set some personal goals. A few things I wanted to accomplish were reading for pleasure more, becoming healthier, and finally releasing my book into the world. I previously began my book but had writer's block off and on for several years. Changing my thinking and viewing lockdown as time to get things done, I prayed and asked a friend to become my accountability partner and help me reach my goals.

TECORA HARVEY

I wasn't sure my friend would be interested in becoming accountability partners because I had no idea about her short and long-term goals. Even though I knew, like me, she believed in the power of prayer, I didn't know about her pandemic struggles. What I did know was that my friend had amazing energy, the ability to replace sobs with laughter, and was always encouraging. My friend agreed to becoming accountability partners, so we decided to have weekly happy hour phone calls on Saturday or Sunday evenings for 15 to 30 minutes. We did goal setting for each upcoming week, as well as shared wins and anything that we needed extra prayer or support with. This included the adventures of homeschooling we both had to tackle. We were kind with ourselves and one another. One week, my goals were simply to get up half an hour earlier and drink more water for seven days. During that week, I'd check my phone and smile at my friend's texts or audio messages throughout the day. I chuckled one day after reading one of her texts because I was staring at my third cup of coffee before lunchtime. After seeing that text, I pushed my mug to the side and picked up my water bottle. My friend ended a relationship during quarantine and moved out on her own. One week, her goal was just to be okay and accept **life**. That week, I sent her texts asking about her well-being, state of mind, and how her reading was coming along.

We acknowledged wins with comments like "Yas, girl!" (Of course, it was in one of the real housewives' tones). Failures and struggles were acknowledged as delayed blessings. We expected some along the way, but we chose not to stay emotionally stuck. Whatever we didn't achieve during any given week, we decided on hitting the ground running and completing the following week. As my friend and I began to trust one another, we became more transparent. Our calls that started out lasting up to 30 minutes soon continued for almost one hour each time.

My friend and I killed it as accountability partners! In spite of a pandemic, we both became healthier and happier. She found the courage to release her comedy skits and other blogs to the world, be okay with ending a relationship that was no longer serving her, and appreciate alone time. I found the courage to create and share this book with you.

Generally as women, we thrive in community. One of the things that will help you heal and overcome personal loss is stepping out of your comfort zone to ask someone who you respect to become your accountability partner. This is an opportunity for you and your partner to support and encourage one another when life seems like it's too much to deal with. Even when life is great, an accountability partner can celebrate the victories with you.

It's often when we are at our lowest that it's most beneficial to get an accountability partner. You might be thinking, *I'm having a really hard time. I'm stuck on this thing. I'm challenged.* From there, you get frustrated or become distant, disconnected, or disinterested in life. When this happens, think about that one person who is close to you. It's the person who has always been a listening ear and offered words of support during your toughest trials. That individual, whether a family member, friend, or religious leader, has already been acting in the role of an accountability partner to you. Now, you both can formalize the relationship, reciprocate the act, and be a source of strength for each other.

My sister is also a wonderful source of strength for me. Whenever I need to release my feelings or concerns about parenting, I look to her because, to me, she is a great example of what it means to survive. After becoming a teen mom, she raised a wonderful, intelligent daughter on her own. My sister and I allow ourselves to be transparent and learn from one another. We share helpful resources and tips and laugh about the silly things our kids put us through. Even though she is younger than me, I call her to get her opinion, at times, about how I could handle challenges with my teenagers. My sister has been a parent longer, so I appreciate that she is more experienced when dealing with some matters.

Often, when I am going through a difficult time, I tend to self-isolate. Is this true for you? Now, you could do this consciously or unconsciously. Regardless, it is not helpful because it's actually counterproductive to your healing. Yes, there will be periods in your life when you need some alone time. We all have moments when we just need to get close to God and figure some things out. But, I've found that disconnecting from the world and self-isolating allows an opening for untruths to negatively influence my thinking. Again, this does not help us heal. You are beautiful, important, loved, desired, cherished, deserving of happiness, and special.

One of the biggest misconceptions, we, as women, have is that we must heal alone. **Life** happens. We go through things and don't know where to begin to look for solutions. That is okay! Although it can be hard to make yourself vulnerable and share your struggles, it helps to identify someone in your life who can be a great mentor or supporter on your journey. This could be a pastor, first lady, therapist, friend, or relative. This person can help you start making sense of some of the feelings you experience and set obtainable goals.

Celebrities may have fame and fortune but many know the importance of surrounding themselves with people who genuinely care for them and will hold them accountable. During her powerful 2018 speech at the Essence Black Women in Hollywood event[3], comedian and actress, Tiffany Haddish, thanked her friends who had always been there for her. Haddish promised to take them all over the world and recounted the period prior to her Hollywood success when she was homeless in California and living in her car. Haddish could have chosen to hide her struggles from those closest to her, but she didn't. Instead, she opened up and allowed her friends to see her situation for what it was. They were in her corner and spoke positivity into her life. We all need these types of friends.

---

[3] Davis, Rachaell. "ESSENCE Black Women In Hollywood Awards: See Tiffany Haddish's Inspiring Acceptance Speech That Left The Whole Room Smiling." ESSENCE. 4 March 2018, https://www.essence.com/awards-events/red-carpet/black-women-hollywood/tiffany-haddish-black-women-hollywood-speech/.

REFLECTION

Do you have someone in your corner to hold you accountable? If so, is your communication as consistent as you'd like?

If you do not have an accountability partner, seek out someone and make contact with the person as soon as possible. Discuss how you will connect. Face-to-face, by phone, via Facetime or Zoom? How often will you have accountability meetings? Once a week, bi-weekly, monthly, or quarterly?

_____

_____

_____

_____

_____

CHAPTER THREE
INCORPORATE ACTS OF GRATITUDE INTO YOUR DAILY ROUTINE

"Gratitude unlocks the fullness of life. It turns what we have into enough, and more. It turns denial into acceptance, chaos to order, confusion to clarity."
- Melody Beattie[4]

Gratitude refers to the state of being thankful and content in life. It aids our self-esteem, emotions, communication, friendships, relationships, stress reduction, optimism, patience, healing and so much more. It motivates you to appreciate others and treat them with kindness. Sometimes saying or journaling a simple *thank you* almost instantly allows you to exhale.

In 2014, I survived the "death of a dream" a.k.a. divorce. I was the woman who hoped beyond hope. I told myself that my kids would only experience being raised in a two-parent household, unlike myself. You can do everything in your power to attempt to make a relationship work but, sometimes, enough is just enough. Life really is bigger than our wants, needs, and what we think it should look like. It's about our God-given purpose, plain and simple. Each of us was created from nothing by God to complete very specific and intentional tasks in life even before we figure them out. We are all unique and special. No other person can do the things you do like you can.

When I was going through my divorce, it was challenging to figure out so many things seemingly overnight, such as where

---

[4] "Melody Beattie Quote - Gratitude." *Oprah.com*, 15 Dec. 2020, http://www.oprah.com/quote/melody-beattie-quote-gratitude.

to live, transportation to get my children and myself around, how to earn more money, and ways to effectively parent alone. I had all this on my plate, and I had to find ways to function every day while experiencing depression, anxiety, and grief. When I got frustrated, I made it a point to stop and thank God for all of my blessings. I thanked Him that my children were safe. I thanked Him for giving me everything I needed. I thanked Him for answering my midnight prayers for *deliverance*. I thanked Him for a divorce process that hadn't resulted in unreasonable compromises regarding parental rights. My children were fortunate that they didn't have to spend three days with me, three days with their father, and alternating holidays between us both. This was something to be truly thankful for.

Despite where you are in your healing process, it helps to stop and simply give thanks for what you do have, what is working in your favor, and that you woke to a new day. Outwardly express gratitude for the things that you may take for granted or don't often acknowledge. These things include running water that's safe to drink, a functioning fridge filled with food, a car that starts every day, the family member who gives you relief when you need a mommy break, someone to care for your child(ren) when there's an emergency, warm shelter, the ability to think rationally, and people who love and support you. Even though the personal loss you're dealing with is great, there *are* certainly things working in your favor. Be thankful for them and for the new mercy you receive each morning.

Not taking time out of your day to thank God for what you have may prevent you from seeing all the miracles and blessings you consistently receive. We sometimes overlook them because we become too focused on what we don't have. If we're constantly in a state of need, how will we recognize when we actually have everything we really need? Much like on Thanksgiving Day, a time when many families gather and put aside offenses that happened during the year, we must shift our energy and spend more time in appreciation for our many blessings.

ACTS OF GRATITUDE YOU CAN DO DAILY

- Say something kind or encouraging to someone else. "You have on a beautiful top" or "I love the way you are patient with your child," goes a long way.
- Do something nice and thoughtful for someone else. Before you head to the grocery store, call and ask a friend or relative that may not get out often if they need anything.
- Hug someone. Some people can count on one hand how many hugs they receive in a year.
- Show someone your beautiful smile.
- Be a listening ear for someone. Someone may appreciate just knowing that you care.
- Be a little more patient with someone.
- Celebrate someone else's victory with them. You can do this via text or sending a message on social media.
- Send someone a "Thinking of You" or "Thank You" card. You can usually pick up two cards for $1 at a local dollar store. After paying for postage, it will cost you less than $2 to bring a smile to someone's face anywhere in the continental U.S.

- Journal. This is a great way to be reminded of how blessed you are.
- Apologize. We may find it hard to apologize. However, when we do so, we remind someone that they are valuable and their voice is important.
- Pay it forward for someone else. Pay for the coffee of the person in the car behind yours. You can also pay the difference for the stranger at the grocery store who is a little short at the register.
- Leave a larger tip for the waiter, waitress, or barista the next time you visit your favorite restaurant or coffee shop.
- Host virtual or in-person meetings with friends just to simply talk and check-in.

No matter the trauma or personal loss you've experienced, showing gratitude aids your healing journey.

REFLECTION

Do you have resources that help you daily express gratitude? What are they? A journal? A playlist?

If you don't have any resources, I suggest you create a gratitude playlist to jam to whenever untruths or overwhelming thoughts start to creep in. Be sure to include songs that will put a smile on your face in the car, while you're cooking, when you're cleaning, and when you're having stressful days.

I've included my favorite playlist in the back of this book. It totally helps me heal.

You can also begin or continue to consistently journal every day.

_____

_____

_____

_____

_____

_____

PART TWO
THERAPY IS FOR YOU

CHAPTER FOUR
WORK WITH A PROFESSIONAL

Tyler Perry's *Acrimony*[5] is a thriller about a devoted wife, Melinda (played by Taraji P. Henson), who seeks revenge on her ex-husband, Robert. Prior to marriage, Melinda discovered her then-boyfriend, Robert, was cheating on her. In a fit of rage, Melinda rams her SUV into Robert's trailer while he is in there with another woman. As the pattern of violence continues, Melinda eventually speaks to a therapist, decades later, about her behavior. Melinda rejects the therapist's clinical suggestion that she may have borderline personality disorder. After hearing those three words, Melinda immediately associated the possible diagnosis to being "crazy."

Unfortunately, many of us still equate mental health struggles with negative stigmas. Mental health awareness is even viewed as a weakness, by some, rather than a strength. I want you to ask yourself: Who is in for the bumpier ride, the person conscious of their mental health or the one in denial about it? Please be mindful that we all have challenges. Most have experienced some form of personal loss or trauma and aren't aware of how they are still affected by it. A professional therapist can help with this.

Melinda was so emotionally scarred by Robert's infidelity that she was unable to see how it affected her behavior. Because of this, and subsequent events in the movie, her overall quality of life decreased as her hostility and violence intensified.

---

[5] Acrimony. Written, Produced and Directed by Tyler Perry, performance by Taraji P. Henson, Tyler Perry Studios, 2018.

Although you may not be one to go to the extreme of getting behind the driver's seat of your car and running into your partner's home, you may have open emotional wounds that take away from you living a happy life.

A common type of mental illness is depression. Depression creates feelings of sadness and disinterest in life and/or activities you may have once enjoyed. If you're depressed, you may feel sad, fatigued, worthless, helpless, or guilty more often. You may also not want to do much of anything, sleep well, or have a desire to live. If you have experienced these feelings, you are not alone. In fact, more and more celebrities and influencers are paving the way by coming out and publicly sharing their mental health battles to normalize the struggles they endure. According to the World Health Organization, "Depression is a common illness worldwide, with more than 264 million people affected...between 76% and 85% of people in low-and middle-income countries receive no treatment for their disorder."[6] In America, quality medical care and resources are more accessible than in third-world countries, yet many people are still unwilling to give therapy a try.

Prior to my first therapy session, I expected to go into a dull office, sit on a couch and go on and on about all of the problems in my life. The first time I actually sat in a therapist's office was during my freshman year at Northern Michigan University. The session actually went nothing like I envisioned; it was casual and relaxed. Student Services offered counseling services free of charge to students, so I decided to try it out. Initially, I had no clue about how to make an appointment or pick a therapist. I didn't even know that there could be focus and goal setting at sessions.

---

[6] "Depression." Who.int, 16 Dec. 2020, www.who.int/news-room/fact-sheets/detail/depression.

TECORA HARVEY

At the time, I recall feeling emotionally overwhelmed prior to the end of my freshman year. Academically, I was good. The issue was that I didn't believe I was transitioning well from being sheltered to making many decisions on my own. I wasn't confident in my decision-making abilities and felt uncomfortable because my peers hadn't experienced some of the things I had. I couldn't name one student I encountered who, like me, knew what it was like to lose a parent as a child. Even though I appeared fine, I thought daily about what it would be like if my mom was present to share my college experience with me. What if she was there to support and encourage me? My grandmother was not able to travel to the upper peninsula of Michigan to help me get settled. Even though my dad and aunt had, I wondered what my grandmother would have thought if she had visited.

I remember being invited to friends' homes for the holidays or on weekends and almost always returning to my dorm room feeling sad because my family life looked nothing like theirs. One afternoon, I had dinner with my academic advisor's family. His daughter and I had a class together. It was really a great experience, and his family showed me that there really were people with big hearts in the world. Yet and still, the experience was just a reminder of an unfamiliar lifestyle. When I finished classes for the day, I usually grabbed a bite from the food court, took a nap, studied for a few hours, then called my grandmother. There was no one waiting to ask how my day was, what I learned, what I enjoyed, etc. If I wanted to talk about these things, I had to reach out to tell someone.

There are many stereotypes about what it means if someone goes to therapy. At the top of the list is the notion that people who go to counseling are crazy. If no one else has told you, Sis,

I'm telling you right now that you are not crazy for getting professional help from a therapist. In fact, I'd say you are more self-aware and wise for taking care of your mental health. Speaking with a therapist can significantly improve the quality of your life and help you uncover the root of many behaviors that may be hindering you.

I had beneficial therapy experiences in college. I learned that it was okay and normal to feel what I was feeling after the trauma I had been through. My therapist never looked at me and told me that I was weak or that I should just "suck it up." She never diminished my traumas or made them seem like mine were less significant than what others went through. She never made any passive remarks about my experiences.

It wasn't actually until I was in my early 30s that the complexity of my past traumas were validated by a professional. Prior to that, it had been like I was moving around separate boxes, from one room to the next, without realizing they belonged in the same room. I struggled with depression for years mostly as a result of my mom committing suicide when I was 10 years old, my grandmother passing, and the years I spent on the receiving end of domestic violence. Even though these are each separate personal losses and traumas, reflecting on one often triggered another. I didn't usually heal from one independent of the other. In conversations with my therapist, I realized these moments were when my depression came back even stronger. They forced me to sit alone and flush out what I really was feeling. I had to ask myself, "What are you really afraid of? What do YOU need? How do you get emotionally unstuck?"

Grief is considered the experience of deep sorrow. If you have lossed a loved one, your grieving period may last longer than you expect. You may feel things that surprise you. You may find it challenging to accept or embrace change. You might even suffer in silence, be unaware of the help you need, or take measures to avoid seeing an actual therapist.

I can recall days and months after my grandmother passed when I would google things like "what happens to your body after death" or "what happens to your soul." Yes, these questions had been addressed in church, but I was in search of very specific, detailed answers. I wanted to read scientific theories. I was interested in spiritual explanations, so I read articles posted online by hospice facilities. I wanted to envision what my grandmother was up to during the nostalgic moments. I wanted a better understanding of what happened once this life ended. It was my way of processing everything because there were moments when I simply could not wrap my head around all the trauma I'd endured.

In the black community, someone might say, "You don't need therapy...that's for white people. Just speak to your pastor." Let me be clear: there is nothing like a praying pastor and first lady who can reference helpful scriptures when you're feeling like an Israelite in Egypt (Exodus 1:13-14, 3:7, and 6:9).[7] Oftentimes, especially for someone raised in church culture, a pastor may fill in the role of a counselor. However, not all pastors are trained in psychology. Yes, you should go to your pastor for spiritual counseling, but chronic depression and mental health struggles are best treated by a professional therapist. This person is equipped with advanced tools such as medication and more long-term approaches.

---

[7] The Holy Bible. King James Version. Red Letter Edition, Barbour Publishing, Inc., 2012.

Church-based therapy and support groups (such as a single's ministry or grief support group) are great during your healing journey. However, if it becomes necessary to get a professional on board, please do not hesitate to do so. A therapist received special training to diagnose and treat you. Yes, opening up to a complete stranger about your trauma, abuse, personal loss, or inner pain can be difficult. However, the healing that comes from releasing all that suffering benefits you so much more.

Identify your triggers. Remember this phrase because it is one of the benefits of working with a professional therapist. My depression used to always get worse around the holidays, especially Thanksgiving and Christmas. Can you envision a train coming your way at full speed? Can you imagine trying to slow it down or stop it just before it knocks you down? Around Thanksgiving, I'd yearn for my mother's side of the family to put their differences aside and enjoy one another for one day. It was bittersweet thinking because, even if we did come together, I knew it would never be as it was when my grandmother was alive.

There were times when I was invited to a friend's house for Thanksgiving; I didn't have to deal with my family around this time. Sometimes I went, but other times I didn't. It all just depended on if I needed alone time to reflect in peace, wanted to succumb to my depression, or desired to be in the company of others. Most often, I opted to stay home for Thanksgiving, allowing myself to feel whatever I was feeling. The holiday would seemingly begin on a happy note but, by nightfall, I was behind my bedroom door numb, angry, and sobbing.

Because of my depression being augmented around the holidays, I would become angry for no logical reason that I had been invited somewhere to spend time with someone else's family instead of my own. I wondered if the invitations were extended to me for ulterior motives. Didn't people know that some of us needed to grieve on holidays centered around families coming together? Unable to control my thoughts and emotions, I succumbed to my anger because it seemed like no one truly thought about me and what I was going through on Thanksgiving. I was upset that, even though it had been years since my mother and grandmother passed, I still heavily grieved for them. My depression caused me to become irate because I didn't know when my unexplained anger would cease—if it ever would.

Once upon a time, being depressed at Christmas was a beast I regretted facing. The weeks leading up to, during, and after Christmas were insufferable. Everything around that time reminded me that my grandmother was no longer with me on this earth. When I saw wrapping paper, I thought about how nice and neat my grandmother wrapped each gift with care. Seeing butter cookies in a tin can reminded me of how my grandmother kept a can of cookies on the living room table in December. Garland reminded me of how my grandmother decorated all the door frames on the lower level of her house. The worst was the endless Christmas movies shown on TV. Watching classics like *A Christmas Story* or *This Christmas* always left me in tears.

After some time of giving in whenever depression hit me around the holidays, I finally decided to do something about it by recognizing my triggers. I have benefited from many years of therapy, and I'll tell you that triggers may be something you need to be conscious of in the long-term. You'll need to learn to reduce or address them in a healthy way. I may have moments of grief during the holidays, but I know to look out for them and have learned how to begin new traditions with my family. In recent years, I've hosted holiday dinners and enjoyed potlucking with a lot of family members. I preserve my grandmother's memory around the holidays by choosing to smile, enjoy and appreciate classic holiday movies, and embrace joy during the holidays, not sadness.

If you're interested in beginning your therapy journey but don't know where to start, I've included some resources for you below.

HOW TO FIND A THERAPIST

- *Psychology Today* is a magazine with tips and resources centered around mental health. On the website, www.psychologytoday.com, you can enter your zip code in a search bar and find local therapists.
- Ask your primary care physician for a referral.
- Get a good referral from someone in your social circle.
- The Federally Qualified Health Center offers therapy on a sliding scale. Visit www.fqhc.org for more information and to locate a center.

REFLECTION

Do you have a therapist? How often do you connect with him or her? Is it enough?

If you don't have a therapist, commit to contacting one within the next seven days. Be sure to check out the resources on the previous page if you're not sure where to start.

_____

_____

_____

_____

_____

CHAPTER FIVE
THE TYPE OF THERAPY MATTERS

If you have chronic stomach issues, you'll probably make your way to a gastrointestinal doctor's office at some point. If you have persistent migraines, there may come a time when you visit a neurologist. If you have problems with your skin, you will likely dial up a dermatologist. This same logic applies when addressing mental health. If you have mental or emotional difficulties, working with a therapist is the way to go.

Who you choose to counsel you matters. Decide if you're more comfortable with a man, woman, Christian, atheist, scientologist, vegan, etc. I've always sought out therapists who I believe could relate to my life experiences. My preference has been someone who is spiritual and a mom. For me, receiving counsel from someone whose practices and beliefs are faith-based is extremely important.

There are different therapy options. Group therapy is a shared therapeutic experience, rather than an individual-based one. In group therapy, patients are able to share with and learn from others with similar experiences or mental health issues. Cognitive behavioral therapy analyzes patients and their connections between thoughts, feelings, and behavior. This therapy is often done with a single therapist. Psychoanalytic therapy focuses on a therapist's long-term approach to treating a chronic mental illness and behaviors that negatively impact the ability to enjoy life. This can include obsessive-compulsive disorder (OCD), anxiety, etc.

Here is a chart that will allow you to brainstorm which therapy you may benefit from the most.

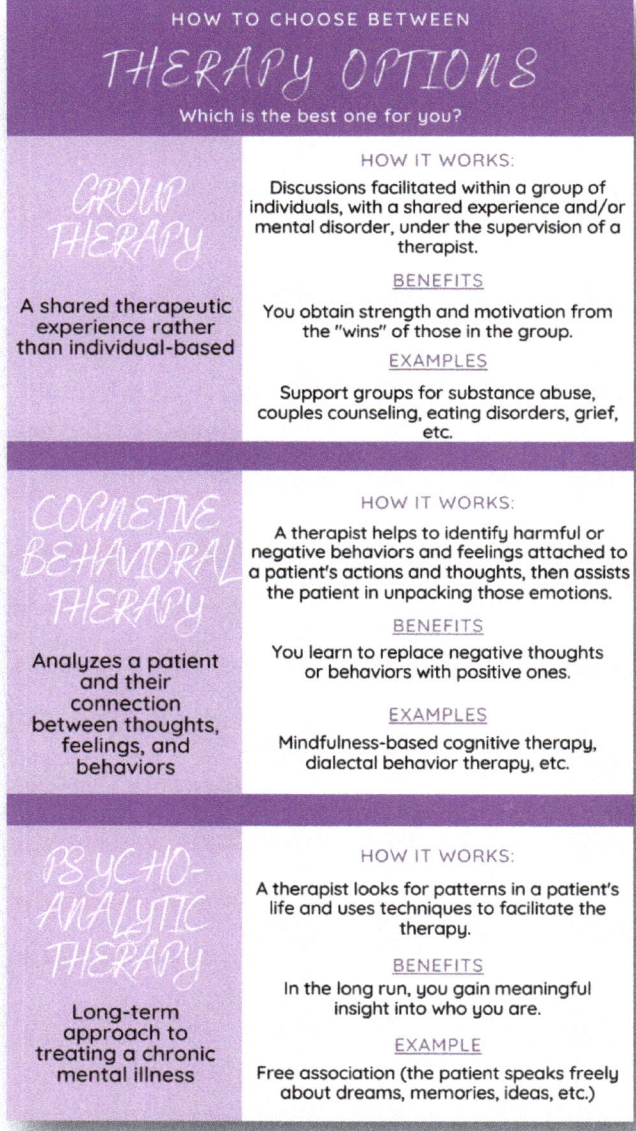

If you suffer from depression, post-traumatic stress disorder (PTSD), bipolar disorder, generalized anxiety, etc., therapy can improve the quality of your life. You could move from a space of hopelessness to thriving and looking forward to new days.

A misconception many people have is that they are only supposed to stay with one therapist for the rest of their lives. This is far from the truth. Depending on where you are in your healing, you can outgrow a therapist and need to work with someone else. Also, you may need a therapist who specializes in specific types of trauma.

When I decided to view myself as a domestic violence survivor, rather than a victim, I had sessions with a therapist who specialized in domestic violence. She was familiar with the barriers and challenges many survivors faced. If you've endured years in a toxic relationship, you first have to develop a new way of thinking. You have to believe that you are worthy of the love and companionship you desire. I began by becoming more aware of any absolutes I was hanging on to. For instance, if there was a relative I hadn't spoken to in years, I began repairing that relationship with a simple phone call. I had to end patterns of self-isolation and remind myself that I had support.

Once I realized that I had achieved my therapy goals, I transitioned to working with a therapist who provided mindfulness counseling. I decided to shift to goal setting focused on parenting because I desired to become a happier, healthier, and more emotionally-present parent.

REFLECTION

Take a minute to think about which type of therapy will be most beneficial to you.

If you have already begun your therapy journey, is there an additional type of therapy you'd like to try?

_____

_____

_____

_____

_____

CHAPTER SIX
BE CONSISTENT

Therapy is not something that's done once or twice. Because the hurt and pain we experience impacts us on deep levels, it often takes months and years to heal. Oftentimes, after seeing a therapist for a few sessions, you may begin to feel better and decide that you no longer need the services.

No matter what you're dealing with in life, consistency matters. This is the same for tending to your mental health. It's important to remain realistic about what going to therapy may look like. Although this is different for everyone, keep in mind that choosing to deal with your trauma may lead to a season of disappointment, hurt, or pain because you will likely have to relive the experiences in order to move past them. We don't necessarily choose our traumas, but we can play a vital role in how we heal from pain and loss. Regardless of what might be waiting for you after you take the step toward healing, know that it is one of the best decisions you will make.

Chapter seven is dedicated to ways you can participate in therapy, even when your money is funny. There may be times when you simply do not feel up to going to a therapy session or two. After all, it can be emotionally draining. Which scenario is more emotionally tolling: dragging yourself to a therapy session when you don't feel up to it or being unable to have therapy as an option because you're in breakdown mode or stuck in bed for days? This is just to give you an idea of what to expect, but we'll touch more on it later.

When I was dating immediately after my divorce, I realized the relationship wasn't a good fit. There was a period where my life was thrown off, and I realized I was in bed for days due to depression. In hindsight, I realized things were off with me because I was not consistently seeing my therapist. I had not reached a point where I could identify many of my triggers and apply the tools I had learned from her yet, so I still needed to see her and work through my struggles. The minute I focused back on therapy, I was easily able to make healthy decisions that were best for me.

By going to therapy, I've learned how to develop more patience with my two teenage daughters. When I first shared this goal with my therapist, we went over how I was communicating with my teens. Yelling was never the goal, but it was a frequent tool. Now, as a result of awareness, I am able to refrain from responding to every remark my daughters make. This was challenging in the beginning because I didn't recognize it as pattern behavior, but I eventually realized that every rebuttal they made did not require a comeback. I am their mother and the person responsible for their well-being. As teenagers, their hormones are all over the place, they go through their identity crises, and they challenge just about everything. Because I was the same way when I was their age, I consistently practice being patient with them. They are going through their own self-development process.

Because consistently going to therapy is a commitment, you may become frustrated with the process and/or lack of progress. You may experience an overwhelming surge of emotions and become exhausted. In spite of these feelings, please resist the urge to stop going to sessions. You want to avoid a cycle of needing to perpetually re-heal. If that's the case, you might want to learn about your triggers and behavioral patterns as soon as possible so that you are well aware of things you struggle with.

REFLECTION

Write down your short and long-term therapy goals. What would you like to achieve in the next few weeks? Six months? One year? Five years?

_____

_____

_____

_____

_____

_____

CHAPTER SEVEN
INVESTING IN YOUR MENTAL HEALTH

*"If you're not feeling good about you,
what you're wearing outside doesn't mean a thing."*
Leontyne Price[8]

I've often heard it said that people do not go to therapy to address their trauma because it's expensive. Many believe they cannot afford therapy, so they never deal with traumatic experiences in their lives properly.

There have been times when my therapy sessions were not covered by my health insurance provider. In those times, I was fortunate enough that I could pay out of pocket for services. Even though it was a financial sacrifice on many occasions, I continued meeting with my therapist consistently because I knew stopping would push me several steps backward. To do so, I restructured my monthly budget as needed. During a month when I scheduled multiple sessions, I eliminated getting my nails done and limited my trips to gourmet coffee shops. If needed, I went to CVS and purchased some good quality nail polish and saved myself at least ten to twenty dollars. Also, I began brewing my own coffee at home more often to save about four dollars per cup.

I didn't worry about the long-term cost of therapy because that would have probably made me talk myself out of paying for it. Instead, I took everything month by month. Some months,

---

[8] Pine, Joslyn. Book of African-American Quotations. E-book, Dover Publications, 2012.

you may need multiple sessions, but others you may not. Similarly, some years you may need more therapy sessions than others. Please do not avoid therapy because you're afraid of the cost. Depending on your specific situation, some therapists may even be able to offer you a discount. If you don't have health insurance, then openly communicate with the therapist to discover alternative options that may be available to you. I shared some options in chapter four. If you have health insurance, the first step is to find out if your therapy visits are covered. If they are, ask about the copay amount you'd be expected to pay at each visit.

Have you ever heard someone say "therapy is a luxury"? Have you said it yourself? Therapy is **not** a luxury. It is a necessity! Therapy isn't only for those who are wealthy, white, or educated. It is for the broken and unhealed. We all have flaws, insecurities, and idiosyncrasies that prevent us from identifying and uprooting the cause of our inner turmoil.

Have you ever been asked a question by someone, given your answer, then had your response blown out of proportion? That person connected your response to something that occured days, weeks, or years earlier that you had no idea about when you replied. Have you ever answered a question, then had someone tell you that what you said offended them? Did their reaction and response leave you shaking your head and feeling mostly bothered by the conversation? Both scenarios are great examples of how we all have tough stuff we need to work on. It could be as simple as misinterpreting a response or taking something personally that has nothing to do with you.

Therapy is an investment that has an invaluable payout. You may not see the return on your investment immediately, but it will come on the day you realize that something that once bothered you hardly does anymore. Here are some things that used to get me emotionally stuck but no longer do:

- Being compared to someone else whose life experiences do not reflect mine. Now, I focus on becoming the best version of myself. I tune out noise.
- Having to make tough relationship decisions. Today, I remain clear about my needs and whether love, respect, and kindness are part of the equation.
- Awaking to a laundry list of tasks. My motto is "slow and steady." It's better to focus and get two things off the list done than to not try and accomplish nothing.

Once you reach the point where certain things no longer bother you, then you can proudly say that you have reached a milestone in healing.

REFLECTION

If you expect to begin therapy soon, find out how much it will cost. Which option is best for you?

If you regularly attend therapy, make sure that you include any portion you cover in your monthly budget of expenses.

If you do not currently attend therapy but would like to start, what can you cut back on to make the investment?

_____

_____

_____

_____

_____

PART THREE
SET HEALTHIER BOUNDARIES

CHAPTER EIGHT
DON'T BE ACCESSIBLE 24/7

In this day and time, there is an ease of access to just about anyone. We have cell phones, email, and multiple social media accounts. For many, friends and family are just a car ride away. Because of the amount of access we have to others, many of us are most often expected to prioritize someone else's pain or problems.

I struggled with balance for years before I realized that my days needed more structure. I'm talking about work-life balance and almost any other balance you can think of. I had a lot of unnecessary stress due to a lack of balance and organization. It was never a matter of a shortage of time, but it was an issue of how I spent my time. I began to utilize the resources I had—planners, calendars, and journals—and noticed a pattern. I had days when I got a lot of nothing done. During those days, I moved about all day doing everything except the tasks I knew I needed to get done due to a lack of focus.

As I added more structure to my life, I also learned the importance of keeping up with daily tasks. To minimize distractions, I stopped being glued to my phone and prioritized which errands I ran. If I was busy doing something positive for my self-care and the phone rang, I let the call go to voicemail. If I needed to run an errand but knew doing it would make me late to a therapy session or another important appointment, I decided to do the errand the next day. Intentionally planning out my day and adding structure ultimately allowed me to gain more balance in my life.

SURVIVING & THRIVING AFTER THE L

By becoming less accessible, I was able to focus on my needs. We all experience stress and challenges throughout the week. As a mom, partner, daughter, sister, or friend, there will always be someone who needs your help, advice, or expertise. In most situations, the demands and questions being thrown your way can wait. As you navigate healthy behaviors to deal with your trauma and apply them in your life, you will need more time to yourself to heal. Being less accessible will show those around you that you are making your wellness a priority. You will also teach them how to do the same thing.

During the COVID-19 pandemic, I needed to practice balance and make myself less accessible to people. During the beginning months of the pandemic, I went an entire week without hardly taking any phone calls. The switch to homeschooling and working remotely became a lot for me, so I needed to process my next steps and what surviving a pandemic meant for my family. I put my phone on silent, worked remotely, and I relied on email as my main form of communication. I was not mentally able to support many others during this week, and I understood that. Because I knew imbalance would be bad for me, I had to be okay with taking time to myself to process **life** and not being available to meet others' demands. I also took advantage of my pre-scheduled personal days off. This allowed me to take a couple steps back, process everything I was feeling, and load up on self-care.

You can't always be the go-to person. You need to allow others the opportunity to problem solve for themselves, especially when you have experienced personal loss and need to heal. It's okay if you are not emotionally, physically, or financially able to assist someone else for a while.

REFLECTION

What is one new practice you can start implementing today to make yourself less accessible to others and have more time to focus on healing?

What are some polite ways you can communicate your need for personal time when someone asks for your help? Practice saying these phrases in the mirror so that you'll say them confidently when the time comes.

_____

_____

_____

_____

_____

CHAPTER NINE
NO MORE PEOPLE PLEASING

Before we discuss anything in this chapter, I want you to declare these four words: no more people pleasing!

In the African-American community, women are often the managers of the household affairs. A majority of women are taught that they should be able to do all the cleaning and cooking, take care of the children, and ensure everything in the home runs smoothly. This way of thinking probably worked back in the 1940s, 50s, and 60s, but a universal mindset shift has taken place as more women are now part of the workforce. Simply put, many women are not in the home all day or able to solely be homemakers.

The reality is that the global economic situation and increase in the cost of living has required more women to work outside of the home to help their families make ends meet. Although we are working outside of the home, a vast majority of us are still responsible for making sure things in our homes function well. I would say most of my married girlfriends manage their homes as if they were still single. They are hands-on with their kids' homework assignments, prepare most of the meals, and take care of the day-to-day duties.

About five years ago, I agreed to assist with setting up for an event because my friend needed extra volunteers. I didn't want to say "no," even though I should have, because I knew she could use the help. After work on the Friday before the event, I went home and prepared everything my kids and I needed for the weekend. On the day of the event, I got up early to do my makeup, fixed my hair, got dressed, helped my children get together, and made my way to the event. I was under the impression that I would help with setup and leave. However, it turned out that I was supposed to stay and help clean up, too. Because I didn't plan for that, I lost an entire day of productivity. I remember beginning work that following Monday drained, exhausted with no meal prep done, and struggling to do the laundry that night.

Now, when I think about that weekend, I recall an old post from T.D. Jakes that read, "If pleasing other people becomes the goal, you will spend the rest of your life trying to satisfy and you'll never have peace."[9] Saying "yes" to something you don't want to do only causes you mental frustration and anxiety. To avoid this, practice saying "no." This isn't easy because telling someone that you're unable to do something, even though you probably can pull it off, seems like a mean thing to do. But, when we are in the process of moving from grieving to healing, we have to make ourselves the number one priority. The consequence of taking on more than we should may end up being more of a detriment to us than the temporary discomfort of politely declining to help someone.

Not prioritizing your needs will lead to feeling overwhelmed with:
- Your job
- Household
- Relationships
- Family
- Mind

---

[9] @BishopJakes. "If pleasing other people becomes the goal, you will spend the rest of your life trying to satisfy and you'll never have peace." Twitter, 7 Jan. 2015, 9:55 a.m., https://twitter.com/BishopJakes.

REFLECTION

Okay, Lady, take a deep breath. Are you ready? Reflect on something on your calendar next week that you really don't want or need to do. If it's something that someone else can cover, consider backing out of that thing. You can do it.

_____

_____

_____

_____

_____

_____

CHAPTER TEN
STOP APOLOGIZING

Ever felt guilty about telling someone "no"? Ever dreaded delivering this news? Did you delay this task? Did this occurrence take up a lot of your time, energy, and focus?

After telling someone "no" recently, I found myself explaining why I couldn't help. When I was finished, I found myself frustrated about the fact that I was expected to provide an explanation for my decision. Furthermore, I actually gave one. This leads me to this chapter's focus, which is to stop apologizing for the decisions you make. You are responsible for protecting your energy, time, and heart. Iyanla Vanzant said it well when she said, "Every relationship you have is a function of the relationship you are having with yourself...I'm talking to you about your ability to respond productively and powerfully to the experiences that come in your life to teach you more about who you are and who you are not..."[10]

There have been times before when I have gone to the grocery store, had someone else bump into me, then apologized to them. The person would tell me it was not my fault, then I would apologize once again before leaving. Only you know all that you have endured. Don't expect everyone to understand. We all do not have the same life experiences, and we certainly don't have them at the same time. If you need to say "no" to someone, then it is your right to set and enforce the boundaries you need.

---

[10] "Who is responsible if your heart gets broken - The R Spot - Episode 12." YouTube, uploaded by Iyanla Vanzant, 30 Sept. 2020.

I worked with an administrator once and was stopped in my tracks when I heard a comment she made to another co-worker. The co-worker was explaining that she had been ill and that was why she hadn't completed her work. Additionally, she told the administrator that she needed to leave the office immediately. It was as if the woman was not listening while the co-worker was explaining her situation. After the exchange, the administrator glanced over at me, stared me in the eyes, and said, "It's not that I don't care. I just don't have time for it." That moment stuck with me until this very day. They were few words, but they were so very powerful. Those two sentences showed me that the administrator had developed an attitude of not taking things personally. She also did not allow others' issues to impact her.

Have you experienced any of these scenarios below?
- Answered a phone call, then listened to the person on the other end of the line for 10 or more minutes longer than intended?
- Did a favor for someone that lasted more than the 30 minutes or so you originally had to spare?
- Said "yes" to someone and been totally thrown off track about what you needed to accomplish for that day?

When you're committed to your healing process, you cannot allow every circumstance or situation someone else is dealing with to affect you. More often than not, what the next person has going on in their life either has nothing to do with you, is not your responsibility, or simply is too heavy for you to carry. You may even find that what they are experiencing could be an emotional trigger for you. If you don't prioritize the time you need to heal, no one else will.

REFLECTION

Why do you think you tend to apologize for things? Does it stem from guilt, a desire to people please, or something else?

Think about the last time you apologized to someone for something that was beyond your control. What happened during that situation?

Are there some things that you are entertaining or giving unnecessary attention to? If so, what are those things? How can you respond effectively to them in a positive manner?

_____

_____

_____

_____

_____

CHAPTER ELEVEN
YOU ARE YOUR OWN EXPERT

As children, we're often taught to trust the judgment, opinion and reasoning of our parent(s), adults, or older people in general. When we become older, we must remind ourselves at times that we know what we really need.

Have you ever gone clothes shopping with a friend and that person suggested you try on pants that you knew wouldn't look good on you? You know your body, so you might immediately think, *I don't know about this.* Your friend insists that you try on pants, so you agree. In the dressing room, you realize the pants won't go past your mid-thigh, so you give up trying to make them fit. After exiting the dressing room without letting your friend see your wardrobe fail, you give her an I-told-you-so glance. It is a process to learn to trust your instincts and judgment.

My old therapist often sat and listened to me go on about how frustrated I was at times if someone expected an explanation from me when I didn't feel one was necessary. It made me angry that I had to justify my decisions about something that I wanted to do. My therapist patiently listened to me, whether it was for five, ten, or twenty minutes. When I was finished, she simply reminded me that I am the expert of my situation. Those words have stayed with me over the years, so I want to say them to you. You are the expert of your situation.

There could be times during your parenting experience when you're expected to explain certain decisions. It could be something as simple as telling one child "no" to a thing but the other "yes" because you understand they have different maturity levels. As a parent, you know the strengths, weaknesses, and personalities of each child. It's okay if not everyone does. You have to be comfortable with making decisions that are in the best interest of your child(ren). You do not have to justify the choices you make on behalf of your child(ren) because you are the one who is responsible for them. You are the same one who will be there to celebrate their victories or support them through their struggles.

You don't have to keep attempting to explain your personal loss or trauma to someone who has not gone through it because that person may never know what it's like. My mom committed suicide when I was 10 by combining alcohol with sleeping pills. Depending on the person, conversation, and timing, I may or may not share this information. I don't try to explain to someone the challenges that I've experienced in losing a parent at an early age. I know that once I lost her, I dealt with fears of rejection, abandonment, trust, change, and insecurity. I was blessed to have a grandmother who could raise and love me unconditionally.

A few things that I learned about myself are that I prefer quiet car rides or listening to music in the car because it allows me time to process feelings. I also take advantage of opportunities to exercise self-care during breaks throughout the day. Additionally, my evenings usually begin with a shower just before or after dinner, which allows me to unwind for the night.

You become clear on what you need and what works for you after going through trial and error. If you want to decrease moments of feeling overwhelmed, sit and reflect on what brings these moments on. If you don't have the level of peace you'd like throughout your days, ask yourself what things could bring you more peace.

I want you to be open to the possibility that your intuition will help guide you. Stop second guessing yourself because you are capable of making great decisions and the changes you need.

REFLECTION

Write down one small change you would like to make but have been indecisive about. What do you need to do to make it happen?

_____

_____

_____

_____

_____

PART FOUR
INDULGE IN SELF-CARE

CHAPTER TWELVE
GET CLEAR ON WHAT REALLY BRINGS YOU JOY

Eat Pray Love[11] is a movie where Liz (played by Julia Roberts) becomes dissatisfied with her home life, marriage, and career. After divorcing her husband, Liz embarks on a journey of self-discovery and travels to Italy, India, and Bali. The movie also features Viola Davis as Delia. Liz and Delia have a heart-to-heart one day, and Liz tells Delia that she wants to go away for a year to travel around the world. Liz shares that she came to this decision after consistently waking up each morning feeling nothing. Liz decides to focus on herself and commit to becoming happier. She shares with Delia that the appetite she had for food and life is gone. In the end, she not only finds her passion for living again, but she also discovers the kind of romantic relationship she desired.

When you do something that you enjoy, a thing that makes you light up, you're practicing self-care. It could be sitting on the couch with a good book, taking a long bubble bath, or going on a hike. You might even hear someone say getting their hair done is how they practice self-care. Well? It is. Generally, though, that is an experience that happens bi-weekly or monthly. What about things you can do to practice self-care daily? Afterall, problems and stress don't show up on a bi-weekly basis; they happen daily.

---

[11] Eat Pray Love. Directed by Ryan Murphy, performances by Julia Roberts and Viola Davis, Sony Pictures, 2010.

If you find that you can't do something "special" for yourself every two weeks or once a month, there are small things you can do to practice self-care. I do at least 30 minutes of exercise as my daily self-care act. I usually walk, go on a bike ride, or play tennis. Exercise is at the top of my self-care list because one of my goals is better weight management. For me, exercise serves a dual purpose because I get to work on becoming healthier and practicing self-care. Plus, exercise releases endorphins, which help with stress reduction.

It is important to learn ways to exercise self-care to avoid triggers in mental health, be able to process any feelings and grief, and avoid burnout.

HERE ARE SOME HOBBIES OR ACTIVITIES YOU CAN TRY:

- A new recipe
- A new craft
- Studying a language
- Yoga
- Aerobics
- Playing an instrument
- Karaoke
- Painting or drawing
- Learning a new sport
- Journaling

REFLECTION

You get to decide how much self-care you need daily. Do you need ten minutes of reading? Thirty minutes of exercise? An hour to journal? Do you need to sit in silence? What do your self-care needs look like?

_____

_____

_____

_____

_____

CHAPTER THIRTEEN
HEALTH IS NON-NEGOTIABLE

"You only get one body and a man will give all his money to regain his health, so pre-serve your health."
Nathaniel H. Bronner, Sr.[12]

Okay, Sis, what I'm about to tell you may not be pleasant. It's even hard to hear. Sometimes our health suffers because we refuse to adopt a healthier lifestyle. Have you ever gone to a doctor's appointment, been told what changes to make to treat your body better, then never made the modifications? Was this one year ago? Three years ago? Every doctor's visit?

A few years ago, I had my annual physical with my primary care doctor. I had an inkling that it would not produce the best results, but I was dumbfounded when I saw how bad it was. The lab work revealed I had a throat goiter that needed to be biopsied. Initially, I was scared because I had no idea what that would entail. Later, the goiter was deemed harmless. Also, because I tended to have chronically heavy menstrual cycles, I agreed to have a vaginal ultrasound. The results revealed that I had two small fibroids and reconfirmed that I have anemia. After all the poking and prodding that happened that year, I promised my primary care physician and myself that I was going to take better care of myself. I also learned that many women suffer from heavy periods, fibroids, and anemia, which is something we don't always have conversations about. Hopefully, there will be a shift and this begins to change.

---

[12] Pine, Joslyn. Book of African-American Quotations. E-book, Dover Publications, 2012.

Unfortunately, there are far too many *strong* women who suffer because they do not prioritize their health. Most of us know someone who suffers from high blood pressure, high cholesterol levels, or something else that's out of whack. We're often too busy working and running our homes to put our own health needs first. As women, we must stay mindful that our children and loved ones are looking to us as examples. We're not always successful in persuading someone else to prioritize their health when they don't see us doing so.

My grandmother passed in 2010 from congestive heart failure and other complications that stemmed from her being a diabetic for over two decades. Generally speaking, self-care is a practice our parents and grandparents weren't told was an option. In fact, they were probably taught to work, work, work. The price of not exercising self-care can lead to being unhappy, unfulfilled, and unsatisfied with the quality of your life. Self-care means something different for everyone, but it is the practice of doing something that brings you peace and joy.

I recently learned that my grandmother worked at a hotel cleaning rooms when she was younger. This explained why she was so meticulous about the upkeep of her home. I watched my grandmother cook multiple meals daily (there wasn't a huge takeout budget), insist on keeping a clean and tidy home, physically care for her disabled adult son, and raise her grandchildren. She consistently did this up until a few months before her passing—when it was no longer physically possible. I sometimes wonder if she would have lived longer if she knew how to prioritize her health. I think, *What if she lived in a safer neighborhood where she was able to walk daily?* Those questions run through my mind as I recognize that we only have one life and one body.

Now that I'm older, when I reflect on it, I think things like tending to her garden, doing crossword puzzles, watching Tyler Perry plays, and reading her Bible were my grandmother's ways of practicing self-care. Taking care of your health is not just about your physical body; it also involves your mental well-being. You may find it helpful to schedule your "health" appointments in your phone or planner. Each weekend, I sit at my dining room table, desk, or couch, and fill in my activities for the upcoming week in my planner. I note things I need to follow up on, such as making dentist appointments, list the form of exercise I'd like to do each day, and write the minimum hours of reading and writing I plan to do. I intentionally include my obligations and activities that help me center because I want to ensure there is room for them weekly.

REFLECTION

Have you been prioritizing your health? Have you scheduled or gone to your annual exam with your primary care doctor? What is one health goal you can set for yourself to improve within the next 30 days? The next 12 months?

_____

_____

_____

_____

_____

_____

CHAPTER FOURTEEN
QUALITY VS. QUANTITY

Your self-care may look different from day-to-day. Be open to that. If I have a really high stress day, my self-care may look like Netflix and chill. Other days, it may be reading and journaling. I want you to think in terms of life-long self-care habits. This is not something to just temporarily incorporate. Like losing weight, you reach success when you make a lifestyle change. If it comes down to it, I exercise on my lunch break. This way, if I have a busy evening with the kids, I've already gotten my self-care activity in for the day.

I've watched *Being Serena*, a documentary about tennis star, Serena Williams, life before. I can recall being surprised to learn that famous athletes have their own self-care rituals they adhere to. Granted, it could be a part of their physical therapy, but it is a form of self-care nonetheless.

The times in my life where I have struggled or failed in prioritizing my self-care usually had some characteristic of me being inconsistent. I had intentions to exercise but never committed to days, times, a schedule, or the type of exercise I planned to do. I set out to write this book before but never set a deadline or was inconsistent with my writing. I didn't have the proper boundaries in place to preserve my time.

I want you to do something for yourself. Please get really clear on what your self-care goals are. For instance, do you want to become healthier by losing thirty pounds in four months? Are you going to try a new skincare routine for thirty days? Are you going to work on improving your oral hygiene? Will you read more? Are you going to try a new hobby? Whatever it is that is your focus, **write it down. Set reminders** and **alarms in your smartphone** to help you stay on track. Commit to your new journey.

Now that you have clarity, how are you going to track your progress? Are you going to install a fitness app or use the one in your phone that you didn't realize was there? Are you going to reflect on your upcoming schedule at the end of each week? I want you to get really clear on whether you are meeting the goals you set. Determine if you are making progress, slow and steady.

I use up almost every inch of the weekly portions of my planner and cross off things that I accomplish throughout the day. For each day that I exercise for more than twenty minutes, I give myself a smiley face. Yep, you read that right. I encourage myself. The goal is to have at least six smiley faces by the end of the week. If I'm short, then I do an extra thirty or so minutes on a different day that week. I also weigh myself monthly to do a check to ensure that I have not gained weight. If the number on the scale is the same or has gone up a little, then I know that I have to exercise harder.

We often don't accomplish our goals because we lack habits that serve us or are ill-prepared when **life** happens. If taking L's has taught me nothing else, it's that **life** is going to happen. I have yet to meet a person exempt from possibly losing a loved one, encountering financial challenges, dealing with employment changes, being on the brink of a health scare, or having to end a relationship.

Please be kind to yourself. If you know that you have an ill loved one who you've been visiting at the hospital every evening after work, then you may be piling on too much by working out on some weekday evenings. I'd suggest maybe getting up earlier in the week and exercising before the rest of your day begins. This also means that you'll be starting your day by doing something for yourself first. Figure out what works best for you. Do your best to avoid being too exhausted to see about yourself.

REFLECTION

Are there changes you need to make to your self-care routine? If so, write them down. Start implementing them TODAY.

_____

_____

_____

_____

_____

Tecora's Favorite Go-To Resources

Music can aid your healing. Here are a few of my favorite songs on repeat at home and on car rides.

SELF-LOVE/ACCEPTANCE
"Pieces of Me" by Ledisi. This song encourages you to embrace the things that make you unique.

GRATITUDE
"Praise is What I Do" by William Murphy. This song is sure to make you thankful for the good and bad experiences.

"I'm Blessed" by Charlie Wilson (feat. T.I.). This song reminds you that you have survived what you've been through.

HOPE/ENCOURAGEMENT
"My God is Awesome" by Charles Jenkins. This song reminds you that God can move mountains.

"Just Fine" by Mary J. Blige. This song reminds you to surround yourself with positive vibes.

"I Smile" by Kirk Franklin. This song compels you to smile even when it hurts.

"Juicy" by The Notorious B.I.G. This song will encourage you to acknowledge what you have overcome.

"Lose to Win" by Fantasia. This song reminds you that there is hope after the L.

PERSEVERANCE/PEACE

"Won't He Do It" by Koryn Hawthorne. This song reminds you there is victory after each challenge.

"I Made It" by Fantasia. This song reminds you to celebrate that you have survived.

STRENGTH

"Dear Mama" by 2Pac. This song reminds you that brighter days are ahead.

"Shake it Off" by Taylor Swift. This song will encourage you to keep moving forward.

EPILOGUE

Now that you have completed *Surviving & Thriving After the L: 14 Effective Ways to Heal After After Personal Loss*, please wave bye-bye to those old practices, beliefs, and habits that have been counterproductive to your healing. You are now equipped with the tools to start showing up brighter, bolder, healthier, and happier. Your journey may seem uncomfortable, tedious, and never-ending at times. It may even mean you have to start saying "no" to people on a regular basis.

In Part One, you were encouraged to re-establish a strong spiritual foundation because you'll need a higher power on your side to get through life.

In Part Two, you were shown that therapy is for you because your healing is enhanced when a professional gets on board.

In Part Three, it was confirmed that you must set healthier boundaries to do away with unnecessary stressors and triggers.

In Part Four, you were presented with the value of indulging in self-care because it should be at the top of your to-do list, not at the bottom.

I am willing to bet that you were aware of some of the concepts in this book. But, let's be honest, there may not have been a sense of urgency the first time you heard about these topics. Now, however, I hope you will apply what you have learned or relearned. Experiencing trauma and personal loss is messy, inconvenient, and impacts us on levels deeper than we think, but we don't have to succumb to the negative impact these circumstances can have on us. We do not need to stay bound or trapped because healing is possible. Remember, there is life after the L.

Visit www.tecoraharvey.com

For additional resources to
aid your healing.

www.ingramcontent.com/pod-product-compliance
Lightning Source LLC
Chambersburg PA
CBHW062023290426
44108CB00024B/2760